The History

The Dragon Kingdom
Unveiled

Copyright © 2023 by Pema James Dorji and Einar Felix Hansen.

All rights reserved. No part of this publication may be reproduced, stored in a retrieval system, or transmitted, in any form or by any means, electronic, mechanical, photocopying, recording, or otherwise, without the prior written permission of the copyright holder. This book was created with the help of Artificial Intelligence technology.

The contents of this book are intended for entertainment purposes only. While every effort has been made to ensure the accuracy and reliability of the information presented, the author and publisher make no warranties or representations as to the accuracy, completeness, or suitability of the information contained herein. The information presented in this book is not intended as a substitute for professional advice, and readers should consult with qualified professionals in the relevant fields for specific advice.

Introduction to Bhutan 6

Geography and Climate of Bhutan 8

Prehistory and Early Settlements in Bhutan 10

The Arrival of Buddhism in Bhutan 12

The Formation of Early Kingdoms in Bhutan 14

The Rise of the Monarchy in Bhutan 16

The Reign of the First Druk Gyalpo 18

The Establishment of the Dual System of Governance 20

The Emergence of the Penlop System 22

The Role of the Zhabdrung in Bhutan's History 24

The Bhutan-Tibet Relationship in Ancient Times 26

The Arrival of the British in Bhutan 28

The Signing of the Treaty of Sinchula 30

The Bhutan-India Relationship in the 20th Century 32

The Impact of World War II on Bhutan 34

The Development of Bhutan's Economy 36

The Role of Agriculture in Bhutan's History 38

The Impact of Education in Bhutan 40

The Establishment of the National Assembly 42

The Implementation of Gross National Happiness 44

The Role of Buddhism in Bhutanese Society 46

The Traditional Arts and Crafts of Bhutan 48

The Festivals and Celebrations of Bhutan 50

The Architecture of Bhutan 52

The Impact of Tourism on Bhutan 54

Bhutan's Environmental Conservation Efforts 56

Bhutan's Future and its Role in the Global Community 58

Conclusion 60

Introduction to Bhutan

Bhutan, also known as the Kingdom of Bhutan, is a small landlocked country located in the eastern Himalayas of South Asia. It is bordered by China to the north and India to the south, east, and west. Bhutan has a total land area of 38,394 square kilometers and a population of approximately 800,000 people.

The official language of Bhutan is Dzongkha, and the national currency is the ngultrum. The capital city of Bhutan is Thimphu, which is also the largest city in the country.

Bhutan is known for its unique culture and tradition, which is deeply rooted in Buddhism. The country has been able to maintain its distinct cultural identity despite its close proximity to India and China.

The people of Bhutan are predominantly Buddhist, and Buddhism has a significant impact on their daily lives. The country is home to many monasteries and temples, which are considered to be some of the most important religious sites in the region.

Bhutan is also known for its stunning natural beauty, which includes majestic mountains, lush forests, and crystal-clear rivers. The country is home to many rare and endangered species of flora and fauna, making it a popular destination for ecotourism.

In recent years, Bhutan has gained international attention for its unique approach to development, which focuses on

Gross National Happiness (GNH) rather than Gross Domestic Product (GDP). GNH is a holistic and sustainable approach to development that emphasizes the happiness and well-being of the people, the preservation of the environment, and the promotion of cultural values.

Overall, Bhutan is a fascinating and unique country that is worth exploring. From its rich cultural heritage to its breathtaking natural landscapes, Bhutan has something to offer for everyone.

Geography and Climate of Bhutan

Bhutan is a small landlocked country located in the eastern Himalayas of South Asia. The country has a total land area of 38,394 square kilometers and is bordered by China to the north and India to the south, east, and west.

The geography of Bhutan is dominated by the Himalayan mountain range, which includes some of the highest peaks in the world. Mount Jomolhari, which stands at 7,326 meters, is the highest peak in Bhutan. The mountains are also the source of many of Bhutan's rivers, including the Punatsang Chhu, Wang Chhu, and Amo Chhu.

The mountains in Bhutan are covered in dense forests, which are home to many rare and endangered species of flora and fauna. The forests are also an important source of timber and other natural resources for the people of Bhutan.

The climate of Bhutan varies depending on the altitude and location. In general, the country experiences a subtropical climate in the south, while the northern parts of the country are covered in snow and ice.

The monsoon season in Bhutan runs from June to September, and during this time, the country experiences heavy rainfall and high humidity. The winter months, from December to February, are cold and dry, with occasional snowfall in the higher elevations.

The temperature in Bhutan also varies depending on the altitude. The lower elevations in the south are generally warm and humid, with temperatures ranging from 15 to 30 degrees Celsius. The higher elevations in the north are much colder, with temperatures ranging from -5 to 10 degrees Celsius.

Due to its unique geography and climate, Bhutan is home to a wide range of plant and animal species. The country is known for its rich biodiversity and is home to many rare and endangered species, including the Bengal tiger, clouded leopard, and Himalayan black bear.

Overall, the geography and climate of Bhutan play a significant role in shaping the country's culture, economy, and way of life. The mountains and forests provide important natural resources, while the rivers and fertile valleys support agriculture and other industries. The climate, while challenging at times, also supports a diverse range of flora and fauna, making Bhutan a truly unique and beautiful country.

Prehistory and Early Settlements in Bhutan

Bhutan has a rich and complex history that dates back to prehistoric times. While much of this early history remains shrouded in mystery, archaeologists have been able to piece together some of the key events and developments that shaped the early settlements in Bhutan.

The earliest evidence of human settlement in Bhutan dates back to the Stone Age, around 2000 BCE. During this time, hunter-gatherer societies were present in the region, living off the natural resources of the forests and rivers.

Over time, these early settlements began to develop more complex social and economic systems. By the Bronze Age, around 1000 BCE, the people of Bhutan were beginning to engage in agriculture and animal husbandry, which allowed them to establish more permanent settlements.

One of the key developments in the early history of Bhutan was the arrival of Buddhism in the region. According to legend, the Indian saint Guru Rinpoche, also known as Padmasambhava, visited Bhutan in the 8th century and introduced Buddhism to the people.

With the arrival of Buddhism, the people of Bhutan began to develop a rich and complex culture that was based on Buddhist principles. This culture was characterized by a deep respect for the natural world, a commitment to non-violence, and a belief in the power of meditation and spiritual practice.

During the medieval period, Bhutan was divided into numerous small kingdoms and principalities, each with its own unique culture and tradition. These kingdoms were often engaged in conflict with one another, and there was a great deal of political instability in the region.

One of the most important figures in the early history of Bhutan was the Tibetan lama Ngawang Namgyal, who arrived in Bhutan in the 17th century. Namgyal played a key role in unifying the various kingdoms of Bhutan under a single system of governance, known as the dual system of government.

Under the dual system, Bhutan was ruled by two leaders, the spiritual leader, known as the Je Khenpo, and the secular leader, known as the Druk Desi. This system helped to establish a stable and unified government in Bhutan, which remained in place until the arrival of British colonialism in the 19th century.

Overall, the prehistory and early settlements in Bhutan were characterized by a rich and complex culture that was deeply rooted in the natural world and the principles of Buddhism. The arrival of Buddhism and the development of a unified system of governance were key developments that helped to shape the early history of Bhutan.

The Arrival of Buddhism in Bhutan

Buddhism is one of the key cultural and spiritual traditions in Bhutan, and it has played a significant role in shaping the country's history, culture, and way of life. The arrival of Buddhism in Bhutan is a complex and multifaceted event that occurred over a period of several centuries.

According to legend, the Indian saint Guru Rinpoche, also known as Padmasambhava, played a key role in introducing Buddhism to Bhutan. In the 8th century, Guru Rinpoche is said to have arrived in Bhutan and performed a series of powerful spiritual practices and rituals that helped to establish the foundations of Buddhism in the region.

Over time, Guru Rinpoche's teachings and practices became more widely accepted and integrated into the culture and way of life of the people of Bhutan. By the 9th century, Buddhism had become the dominant spiritual tradition in the region, and many monasteries and temples were being built to support the growing Buddhist community.

One of the key features of Buddhism in Bhutan is the unique blend of tantric and traditional Buddhist practices. This blend of practices has helped to create a distinctive Bhutanese form of Buddhism that is characterized by its emphasis on meditation, ritual, and devotion.

Another important aspect of Buddhism in Bhutan is the role of the monastic community. The monasteries and temples in Bhutan serve as important centers of learning, meditation, and spiritual practice. Monks and nuns play a key role in preserving and transmitting the teachings of Buddhism, and many young people in Bhutan are sent to monasteries and temples to receive a Buddhist education.

Buddhism in Bhutan also has a strong connection to the natural world. The principles of Buddhism emphasize the interconnectedness of all things, and this belief is reflected in the way that the people of Bhutan interact with their environment. Bhutan has a strong tradition of environmental conservation, and many of the country's natural resources are protected by law.

Overall, the arrival of Buddhism in Bhutan was a complex and multifaceted event that occurred over a period of several centuries. The teachings and practices of Buddhism have had a profound impact on the culture, history, and way of life of the people of Bhutan, and they continue to play a key role in shaping the country's identity and future.

The Formation of Early Kingdoms in Bhutan

The formation of early kingdoms in Bhutan is a complex and multifaceted event that occurred over a period of several centuries. While much of the early history of Bhutan remains shrouded in mystery, archaeologists and historians have been able to piece together some of the key developments that led to the formation of early kingdoms in the region.

One of the earliest kingdoms in Bhutan was the Lhomon Kingdom, which is believed to have existed around the 5th century CE. This kingdom was located in the eastern part of Bhutan, near the present-day town of Mongar. The Lhomon Kingdom was characterized by a complex social and economic system, which included agriculture, animal husbandry, and trade.

Over time, the Lhomon Kingdom was replaced by other kingdoms, including the Bumthang Kingdom, which emerged in the 7th century CE. The Bumthang Kingdom was located in central Bhutan and was known for its advanced metallurgy and ironworking techniques. The Bumthang Kingdom was also characterized by a rich cultural and religious tradition, which included the development of Buddhist art and architecture.

Other important kingdoms in Bhutan during this period included the Paro Kingdom, the Trongsa Kingdom, and the Punakha Kingdom. These kingdoms were often engaged in conflict with one another, and there was a great deal of political instability in the region.

One of the key developments in the formation of early kingdoms in Bhutan was the arrival of Buddhism. Buddhism played a significant role in shaping the culture and way of life of the people of Bhutan, and it helped to establish a shared sense of identity and purpose among the various kingdoms.

Another important factor in the formation of early kingdoms in Bhutan was the natural environment. Bhutan's rugged terrain and harsh climate made it difficult to establish large and stable settlements, and this led to the development of small, decentralized kingdoms that were spread out across the region.

Overall, the formation of early kingdoms in Bhutan was a complex and multifaceted event that occurred over a period of several centuries. While much of this early history remains shrouded in mystery, the development of these early kingdoms helped to establish a shared sense of identity and purpose among the people of Bhutan, which continues to this day.

The Rise of the Monarchy in Bhutan

The rise of the monarchy in Bhutan is a key event in the country's history that helped to shape its political and social structures. While the exact details of the rise of the monarchy remain somewhat unclear, historians have been able to piece together some of the key developments that led to the establishment of a unified system of governance in Bhutan.

One of the key figures in the rise of the monarchy was the Tibetan lama Ngawang Namgyal, who arrived in Bhutan in the 17th century. Namgyal played a key role in unifying the various kingdoms and principalities of Bhutan under a single system of governance, known as the dual system of government.

Under the dual system, Bhutan was ruled by two leaders: the spiritual leader, known as the Je Khenpo, and the secular leader, known as the Druk Desi. The Je Khenpo was responsible for overseeing the spiritual and religious affairs of the country, while the Druk Desi was responsible for overseeing the secular affairs of the country.

The establishment of the dual system helped to establish a stable and unified government in Bhutan, which remained in place for several centuries. During this time, the country experienced a period of relative peace and stability, which allowed for the development of its unique culture and traditions.

In the early 20th century, Bhutan began to undergo a period of political modernization and reform. In 1907, the first king of Bhutan, Ugyen Wangchuck, was crowned. Wangchuck was a popular and respected leader who helped to modernize the country's government and institutions.

Under Wangchuck's leadership, Bhutan underwent a number of key reforms, including the establishment of a formal legal system, the development of a modern education system, and the expansion of infrastructure and communication networks.

In 2008, Bhutan underwent another significant political development when it transitioned to a democratic system of government. This transition was led by the fourth king of Bhutan, Jigme Singye Wangchuck, who abdicated the throne in favor of his son, Jigme Khesar Namgyel Wangchuck.

Today, Bhutan is a constitutional monarchy with a democratic system of government. While the monarchy remains an important symbol of national identity and unity, the country's government is now led by an elected prime minister and parliament.

Overall, the rise of the monarchy in Bhutan was a complex and multifaceted event that helped to establish a stable and unified system of governance in the country. While the country has undergone many changes since this time, the legacy of the monarchy and the dual system of government remain an important part of Bhutan's history and identity.

The Reign of the First Druk Gyalpo

The first Druk Gyalpo, Ugyen Wangchuck, was a key figure in the early history of modern Bhutan. He played a significant role in unifying the country and establishing a stable system of governance that helped to lay the foundation for Bhutan's unique cultural and political identity.

Ugyen Wangchuck was born in 1862, the son of a local governor in central Bhutan. He began his career in the civil service, serving as a court official and diplomat for the Bhutanese government.

In 1907, following a period of political instability and conflict, Ugyen Wangchuck was elected as the first Druk Gyalpo, or Dragon King, of Bhutan. His coronation ceremony marked the beginning of a new era in Bhutan's history, and it helped to establish the country's unique system of government and monarchy.

During his reign, Ugyen Wangchuck implemented a number of key reforms and initiatives that helped to modernize the country's government and institutions. He established a formal legal system, which helped to establish the rule of law and protect the rights of the people. He also developed a modern education system, which helped to improve literacy rates and provide greater opportunities for the Bhutanese people.

In addition to these reforms, Ugyen Wangchuck also helped to establish Bhutan's international reputation as a unique and special country. He fostered diplomatic relations with neighboring countries, and he worked to preserve and promote Bhutan's unique cultural and environmental heritage.

Ugyen Wangchuck's reign also saw the establishment of the Royal House of Wangchuck, which has since become one of the most respected and revered royal families in the world. Under the leadership of the Wangchuck dynasty, Bhutan has continued to develop and modernize while preserving its unique cultural and environmental heritage.

Today, Ugyen Wangchuck is remembered as a key figure in the history of Bhutan. His legacy as the first Druk Gyalpo has helped to establish a stable and unified system of governance that has helped to shape the country's identity and culture. His contributions to the development of Bhutan's legal, educational, and diplomatic systems have helped to establish the foundations of a modern and progressive society.

The Establishment of the Dual System of Governance

The establishment of the dual system of governance in Bhutan is a key event in the country's history that helped to shape its political and social structures. The dual system of governance was a unique system in which Bhutan was ruled by two leaders, the spiritual leader (Je Khenpo) and the secular leader (Druk Desi).

The dual system of governance was established in the 17th century by the Tibetan lama Ngawang Namgyal, who arrived in Bhutan at a time when the country was characterized by political instability and conflict. Namgyal played a key role in unifying the various kingdoms and principalities of Bhutan under a single system of governance.

Under the dual system, the Je Khenpo was responsible for overseeing the spiritual and religious affairs of the country, while the Druk Desi was responsible for overseeing the secular affairs of the country. The Je Khenpo was a powerful figure who held considerable influence over the people of Bhutan, and his role helped to establish a shared sense of identity and purpose among the various regions and communities of the country.

One of the key features of the dual system was the balance of power between the spiritual and secular leaders. The Je Khenpo and the Druk Desi were equal partners in the governance of the country, and their roles were complementary rather than competitive.

The dual system also helped to establish a stable and unified system of governance in Bhutan, which allowed for the development of the country's unique culture and traditions. Under the dual system, Bhutan was able to maintain its independence and sovereignty, despite being located between two powerful neighbors, China and India.

Today, the dual system of governance remains an important part of Bhutan's political and social structures. The Je Khenpo and the Druk Desi continue to hold important roles in the governance of the country, and they are respected and revered by the people of Bhutan.

Overall, the establishment of the dual system of governance was a key event in the history of Bhutan. It helped to establish a stable and unified system of governance that has helped to shape the country's identity and culture. The dual system remains an important part of Bhutan's political and social structures, and it continues to influence the country's development and future.

The Emergence of the Penlop System

The emergence of the Penlop system in Bhutan is a key event in the country's history that helped to shape its political and social structures. The Penlop system was a feudal system in which the country was divided into various regions, each of which was ruled by a Penlop, or governor.

The Penlop system emerged in the 17th century, at a time when Bhutan was characterized by political instability and conflict. The Penlops were powerful feudal lords who held considerable power and influence over their respective regions.

Under the Penlop system, each region was responsible for its own defense and administration, and the Penlops were given a high degree of autonomy in their governance of their respective regions. This system allowed for the development of local customs and traditions, and it helped to establish a sense of regional identity and pride among the people of Bhutan.

However, the Penlop system was also characterized by a high degree of political instability and conflict. The Penlops were often engaged in power struggles and territorial disputes with one another, and this led to a great deal of violence and bloodshed.

Over time, the central government in Bhutan began to exert more control over the Penlops, and the system became more centralized. The Penlops were required to pay tribute to the central government, and they were required to submit to the authority of the Druk Desi and the Je Khenpo.

Despite these changes, the Penlop system remained an important part of Bhutan's political and social structures for many years. Even today, the legacy of the Penlops is visible in the country's regional identities and customs.

Overall, the emergence of the Penlop system was a complex and multifaceted event that helped to shape the political and social structures of Bhutan. While the system was characterized by a great deal of political instability and conflict, it also helped to establish a sense of regional identity and pride among the people of Bhutan. The legacy of the Penlops remains an important part of Bhutan's history and identity to this day.

The Role of the Zhabdrung in Bhutan's History

The Zhabdrung was a key figure in Bhutan's history who played a significant role in shaping the country's political and social structures. The Zhabdrung was a title given to the leader of the Drukpa lineage of Tibetan Buddhism, and it was first introduced to Bhutan in the 17th century.

The first Zhabdrung to come to Bhutan was Ngawang Namgyal, who was a Tibetan lama and a key figure in the establishment of the dual system of governance. Ngawang Namgyal played a key role in unifying the various kingdoms and principalities of Bhutan under a single system of governance, and his legacy as a unifying figure is still felt in Bhutan to this day.

The Zhabdrung was an important figure in Bhutanese society, and his role was both spiritual and political. As a spiritual leader, the Zhabdrung was responsible for overseeing the religious affairs of the country, and he was considered to be the head of the Drukpa lineage of Tibetan Buddhism in Bhutan.

As a political leader, the Zhabdrung was responsible for overseeing the secular affairs of the country, and he played a key role in establishing a centralized system of governance in Bhutan. Under the leadership of the Zhabdrung, Bhutan was able to maintain its independence and sovereignty, despite being located between two powerful neighbors, China and India.

The Zhabdrung also played a key role in shaping Bhutan's unique cultural and environmental heritage. He encouraged the development of Bhutanese art, architecture, and literature, and he helped to establish a system of environmental stewardship that has helped to preserve the country's natural beauty and biodiversity.

Today, the legacy of the Zhabdrung is still felt in Bhutanese society. While the role of the Zhabdrung has changed over time, with the establishment of a constitutional monarchy and a democratic system of government, the Zhabdrung remains an important figure in the country's cultural and spiritual heritage.

Overall, the role of the Zhabdrung in Bhutan's history was complex and multifaceted. As a spiritual and political leader, the Zhabdrung played a key role in shaping the country's identity and culture, and his legacy is still felt in Bhutanese society to this day.

The Bhutan-Tibet Relationship in Ancient Times

The relationship between Bhutan and Tibet has a long and complex history that dates back to ancient times. The two regions share many cultural and religious similarities, and their relationship has been characterized by both cooperation and conflict.

In ancient times, Bhutan was a part of the Tibetan empire, which exerted a great deal of influence over the region. Tibetan Buddhism was the dominant religion in Bhutan, and many of Bhutan's early rulers were either Tibetans or were closely connected to the Tibetan court.

However, the relationship between Bhutan and Tibet was not always a peaceful one. In the 8th century, Bhutan was invaded by Tibetan forces, and the region was brought under Tibetan control for several centuries. This period of occupation was characterized by a great deal of conflict and instability, and it left a lasting impact on the region.

Over time, the relationship between Bhutan and Tibet began to evolve. In the 17th century, the Zhabdrung Ngawang Namgyal arrived in Bhutan and played a key role in unifying the various kingdoms and principalities under a single system of governance. This system was characterized by a unique blend of Tibetan and Bhutanese cultural and religious traditions.

During this period, Bhutan was able to maintain a degree of independence and autonomy from Tibet, and the two regions maintained a cooperative relationship based on shared cultural and religious traditions. However, this cooperation was not always smooth, and there were periods of conflict and tension between the two regions.

Today, the relationship between Bhutan and Tibet remains complex and multifaceted. While the two regions share many cultural and religious traditions, Bhutan has developed a unique identity and culture that is distinct from that of Tibet. Bhutan has also developed strong ties with neighboring India, which has helped to shape the country's political and economic development.

Overall, the Bhutan-Tibet relationship in ancient times was characterized by both cooperation and conflict. The two regions share many cultural and religious traditions, but their unique identities and histories have also shaped their relationship over time. The legacy of this relationship is still felt in Bhutanese society today.

The Arrival of the British in Bhutan

The arrival of the British in Bhutan in the 19th century marked a significant turning point in the country's history. The British were expanding their colonial empire in South Asia at the time, and Bhutan was one of the few remaining independent states in the region.

The first British contact with Bhutan came in the form of explorers and surveyors who were mapping the region in the early 19th century. In 1772, George Bogle, a British representative, visited Bhutan with the aim of establishing trade and diplomatic relations with the country.

However, it was not until the mid-19th century that the British began to exert more direct influence over Bhutan. In 1865, the British sent a military expedition to Bhutan in response to a border dispute between Bhutan and British India.

The expedition resulted in a treaty being signed between Bhutan and the British, which established British influence over Bhutan's foreign affairs. The treaty also required Bhutan to pay tribute to the British government in exchange for protection from external threats.

The British presence in Bhutan was largely confined to the border areas, and the country was able to maintain a degree of autonomy in its internal affairs. However, the British influence did have an impact on Bhutanese society and culture.

Under British influence, Bhutan began to modernize and develop its infrastructure. The country established its first postal service and telegraph system, and it also began to develop its education and healthcare systems. These changes helped to modernize Bhutanese society, but they also had an impact on the country's traditional way of life.

The British presence in Bhutan began to decline in the early 20th century, as the British colonial empire began to disintegrate. In 1947, India gained its independence from British rule, and Bhutan began to establish closer ties with its southern neighbor.

Today, the legacy of the British presence in Bhutan is still felt in the country's political and social structures. While the country has maintained its independence and autonomy, it has also been influenced by the changes brought about by the British presence. The relationship between Bhutan and Britain remains an important part of the country's history and identity.

The Signing of the Treaty of Sinchula

The signing of the Treaty of Sinchula in 1865 was a key event in the history of Bhutan. The treaty was signed between the British government and the Bhutanese authorities, and it established British influence over Bhutan's foreign affairs.

The treaty was signed following a military expedition by the British to Bhutan, which was prompted by a border dispute between Bhutan and British India. The British forces were able to secure a victory over the Bhutanese forces, and this led to the signing of the treaty.

Under the terms of the treaty, Bhutan agreed to cede control of the Duars region to the British government. The treaty also required Bhutan to pay an annual tribute to the British government in exchange for protection from external threats.

In addition, the treaty established British influence over Bhutan's foreign affairs, and it required Bhutan to seek British approval before entering into any diplomatic or commercial relations with other countries.

The signing of the Treaty of Sinchula had a significant impact on Bhutanese society and culture. The treaty led to the development of closer ties between Bhutan and British India, and it also paved the way for the modernization and development of Bhutanese society.

Under British influence, Bhutan began to modernize its infrastructure and institutions. The country established its first postal service and telegraph system, and it also began to develop its education and healthcare systems.

However, the treaty also had an impact on the country's traditional way of life. The British presence in Bhutan began to erode the country's isolation and autonomy, and it led to changes in the country's political and social structures.

Today, the legacy of the Treaty of Sinchula is still felt in Bhutanese society. While the country has maintained its independence and autonomy, it has also been influenced by the changes brought about by the treaty and the British presence in the region. The relationship between Bhutan and Britain remains an important part of the country's history and identity.

The Bhutan-India Relationship in the 20th Century

The relationship between Bhutan and India in the 20th century was characterized by a close partnership and cooperation. India played a significant role in helping to shape Bhutan's political and economic development, and the two countries developed strong ties based on shared cultural and historical traditions.

In the early 20th century, India gained its independence from British rule, and this led to a shift in the relationship between Bhutan and India. Bhutan began to establish closer ties with India, and the two countries signed a treaty of friendship in 1949, which established India's support for Bhutan's independence and territorial integrity.

Under the treaty, India agreed to provide Bhutan with economic and military assistance, and the two countries began to work together on a range of issues, including economic development, trade, and security.

India played a key role in helping to modernize and develop Bhutan's infrastructure and institutions. India provided technical and financial assistance for the development of Bhutan's road network, and it also helped to establish the country's first airport and hydroelectric projects.

In addition, India played a key role in helping to establish Bhutan's democratic system of government. India provided technical assistance and advice during the drafting of Bhutan's constitution, and it also played a key role in helping to organize Bhutan's first democratic elections in 2008.

The close relationship between Bhutan and India was also characterized by cultural and historical ties. Bhutan and India share many cultural and religious traditions, and this has helped to foster a sense of cooperation and partnership between the two countries.

Today, the relationship between Bhutan and India remains strong and continues to evolve. While Bhutan has maintained its independence and autonomy, India continues to provide support and assistance for the country's political and economic development. The relationship between the two countries is an important part of Bhutan's history and identity.

The Impact of World War II on Bhutan

The impact of World War II on Bhutan was relatively limited, as the country was able to maintain its independence and autonomy throughout the war. However, the war had a significant impact on the broader region, and it had indirect effects on Bhutan's political and economic development.

During World War II, the region that includes Bhutan was a key battleground between British and Japanese forces. The fighting in the region had a significant impact on neighboring countries such as India, which was under British colonial rule at the time.

Bhutan's proximity to India meant that the country was indirectly affected by the war. The war led to shortages of goods and supplies in the region, which had an impact on Bhutan's economy and society. The country was also affected by the political and social changes that were taking place in neighboring India.

However, Bhutan was able to maintain its independence and neutrality throughout the war. The country continued to maintain its unique political and social structures, and it was largely able to avoid the direct impact of the conflict.

In the aftermath of World War II, the impact of the conflict on Bhutan was relatively limited. However, the war did have indirect effects on the country's political and economic development. The shortages and disruptions caused by the war had an impact on Bhutan's economy, and the changes taking place in neighboring India had an impact on the country's political and social structures.

Today, the legacy of World War II is still felt in Bhutanese society. While the country was able to maintain its independence and autonomy during the war, it was indirectly affected by the conflict and the broader changes taking place in the region. The impact of the war is an important part of Bhutan's history and identity.

The Development of Bhutan's Economy

The development of Bhutan's economy has been a gradual process that has been shaped by a range of historical, political, and social factors. Prior to the 1960s, the Bhutanese economy was largely based on subsistence agriculture and trade.

However, in the 1960s, Bhutan began to modernize its economy and develop its infrastructure. The country began to build roads and other transportation infrastructure, and it also established its first hydroelectric projects.

The development of Bhutan's economy has been largely driven by the country's natural resources, particularly its water resources. Bhutan has significant hydropower potential, and the country has developed a number of hydropower projects in recent years.

In addition, Bhutan has developed its tourism industry in recent years, as the country's unique culture and environment has become increasingly popular with tourists from around the world.

The government of Bhutan has played a key role in guiding the development of the country's economy. The government has implemented a range of policies and programs aimed at promoting economic growth and development, including the promotion of private sector development and foreign investment.

Despite these efforts, Bhutan's economy remains relatively small and underdeveloped compared to other countries in the region. The country faces a range of challenges, including limited infrastructure and a lack of skilled labor.

In recent years, the government of Bhutan has placed increasing emphasis on the development of a green economy, which focuses on sustainable development and the preservation of the country's natural environment. The government has also implemented a range of policies aimed at promoting social welfare and reducing poverty.

Today, the development of Bhutan's economy remains an ongoing process. While the country has made significant progress in recent years, there is still much work to be done in order to ensure that the benefits of economic growth are shared by all segments of society. The development of Bhutan's economy is an important part of the country's history and identity.

The Role of Agriculture in Bhutan's History

Agriculture has played a significant role in Bhutan's history and development. The country's rugged terrain and mountainous landscape have historically made agriculture the most viable means of subsistence for the majority of the population.

For much of Bhutan's history, agriculture was based on subsistence farming, with small-scale farmers growing crops such as rice, maize, wheat, and barley. Agriculture was a central part of Bhutanese society and culture, and it played a key role in shaping the country's social and economic structures.

The development of agriculture in Bhutan has been shaped by a range of historical and political factors. Prior to the modern era, agriculture was largely organized around the system of feudal land ownership and tenancy, with powerful landowners controlling the means of production.

In the 1960s and 1970s, the government of Bhutan began to implement policies aimed at modernizing and developing the country's agricultural sector. These policies included the establishment of agricultural extension services, the introduction of high-yield crop varieties, and the development of irrigation infrastructure.

Today, agriculture remains a key part of Bhutan's economy and society. The majority of the population is engaged in agriculture, and the sector accounts for a significant share of the country's gross domestic product (GDP).

The government of Bhutan continues to play a key role in guiding the development of the country's agricultural sector. The government has implemented a range of policies aimed at promoting sustainable agriculture and preserving the country's natural environment.

In recent years, the government has also placed increasing emphasis on the development of organic farming and the promotion of traditional farming practices. The government has established a certification system for organic farming, and it has encouraged the development of agroforestry systems and other sustainable farming practices.

Today, the role of agriculture in Bhutan's history and development remains an important part of the country's identity. While the sector faces a range of challenges, including limited infrastructure and a lack of access to credit and other resources, agriculture continues to play a key role in shaping the country's social and economic structures.

The Impact of Education in Bhutan

The development of education has had a significant impact on Bhutan's society and economy. Education has played a key role in shaping the country's social and political structures, and it has been instrumental in the country's modernization and development.

Prior to the modern era, education in Bhutan was largely limited to religious instruction provided by monastic institutions. However, in the 1960s, the government of Bhutan began to implement policies aimed at expanding access to education and developing a modern education system.

Today, Bhutan has a relatively well-developed education system, with a literacy rate of over 70 percent. The country has made significant progress in expanding access to education, particularly in rural areas where access to education was historically limited.

Education has had a significant impact on Bhutan's social and political structures. The development of a modern education system has helped to break down traditional social hierarchies and promote social mobility. Education has also played a key role in promoting gender equality and empowering women in Bhutanese society.

In addition, education has been instrumental in the country's economic development. The development of a skilled and educated workforce has been essential in the development of Bhutan's hydropower sector and other key industries.

The government of Bhutan continues to place a strong emphasis on education. The country has implemented a range of policies aimed at promoting access to education, including the establishment of a national education system and the provision of free primary education for all children.

However, the education sector in Bhutan still faces a range of challenges. These include limited resources, a shortage of qualified teachers, and a lack of access to higher education for many students. The government of Bhutan is working to address these challenges, and education remains a key priority for the country's development.

Today, the impact of education in Bhutan is an important part of the country's history and identity. Education has played a central role in shaping the country's social, political, and economic structures, and it will continue to be a key factor in the country's development in the years to come.

The Establishment of the National Assembly

The establishment of the National Assembly, or Tshogdu, in Bhutan was a significant event in the country's political history. The National Assembly is the country's main legislative body, and it plays a key role in shaping Bhutan's laws and policies.

The National Assembly was established in 1953 by the country's first king, Jigme Dorji Wangchuck. The establishment of the National Assembly was part of a broader effort to modernize Bhutan's political system and establish a more democratic form of government.

Initially, the National Assembly consisted of appointed members, including representatives from the country's monastic community, aristocracy, and civil service. However, in 1963, the king announced that the National Assembly would be transformed into an elected body.

The first elections to the National Assembly were held in 1965, with voters electing representatives from each of the country's twenty districts. The National Assembly had limited powers at this time, and its main role was to advise the king on matters of policy.

However, in the years that followed, the National Assembly's powers and responsibilities gradually expanded. The National Assembly was given the power to approve the country's annual budget, and it also played a key role in the drafting and passage of new laws and policies.

Today, the National Assembly is a key part of Bhutan's political system. The National Assembly is made up of 47 members, with each member elected for a term of five years. The National Assembly is responsible for approving the country's annual budget, as well as for overseeing the work of the government and passing new laws and policies.

The establishment of the National Assembly was a significant milestone in Bhutan's political history, and it played a key role in establishing a more democratic form of government in the country. While the National Assembly still faces a range of challenges, including limited resources and a lack of political experience among some members, it remains an important part of Bhutan's political system and identity.

The Implementation of Gross National Happiness

The concept of Gross National Happiness (GNH) is a unique development philosophy that was developed in Bhutan in the 1970s. The philosophy seeks to prioritize the well-being of individuals and society over economic growth, and it has had a significant impact on Bhutan's social and economic policies.

The concept of GNH was first introduced by the country's fourth king, Jigme Singye Wangchuck, in the early 1970s. The king believed that economic growth alone was not enough to ensure the well-being of Bhutan's citizens, and he sought to develop a more holistic approach to development that placed greater emphasis on social, cultural, and environmental factors.

The implementation of GNH in Bhutan has involved a range of policies and programs aimed at promoting well-being and happiness. These policies include the promotion of sustainable development, the preservation of Bhutanese culture and traditions, and the promotion of good governance and democracy.

One of the key principles of GNH is the idea that economic development should be balanced with social and environmental development. This has led to policies aimed at promoting sustainable development and protecting the country's natural resources.

Another key principle of GNH is the idea that cultural and spiritual values should be given equal importance to material values. This has led to policies aimed at preserving Bhutanese culture and traditions, such as the promotion of traditional arts and crafts and the preservation of traditional architecture.

The implementation of GNH has also involved efforts to promote good governance and democracy. The government of Bhutan has sought to develop a more participatory and inclusive political system, with a focus on promoting transparency, accountability, and citizen participation.

Today, GNH remains an important part of Bhutan's national identity and development philosophy. The country's government has implemented a range of policies aimed at promoting well-being and happiness, and the concept of GNH has gained recognition and support from the international community.

While the implementation of GNH in Bhutan has been largely successful, it also faces a range of challenges. These include limited resources, a lack of expertise in implementing GNH policies, and a need for greater awareness and understanding of the concept among the Bhutanese people.

Overall, the implementation of GNH in Bhutan has been a significant milestone in the country's history and development, and it has had a significant impact on the country's social, cultural, and economic policies. While challenges remain, the concept of GNH continues to inspire and guide Bhutan's development efforts today.

The Role of Buddhism in Bhutanese Society

Buddhism has played a central role in Bhutanese society for more than a thousand years. The country's official religion is Buddhism, and it is deeply ingrained in the culture, traditions, and daily life of the Bhutanese people.

Buddhism was introduced to Bhutan in the 7th century by the Tibetan king Songtsen Gampo. Since then, Buddhism has become an integral part of Bhutanese culture and identity.

Buddhism in Bhutan is primarily of the Vajrayana tradition, also known as Tantric Buddhism. This tradition emphasizes the importance of spiritual practices such as meditation, visualization, and mantra recitation, and it has played a key role in shaping Bhutanese culture and spirituality.

One of the key aspects of Buddhism in Bhutan is the relationship between the monastic and lay communities. Monks and nuns play a central role in Bhutanese society, and they are highly respected for their spiritual knowledge and dedication to the Buddhist path. Laypeople, meanwhile, support the monastic community through donations and other forms of assistance.

Buddhism in Bhutan has also played a key role in shaping the country's political and social systems. The Bhutanese monarchy, for example, has traditionally been closely linked to the Buddhist religion, with the king serving as the country's spiritual leader as well as its political leader.

Buddhism in Bhutan has also had a significant impact on the country's art, architecture, and literature. Bhutanese art and architecture are characterized by their intricate designs and religious symbolism, and Buddhist themes are prominent in the country's literature and poetry.

Today, Buddhism remains a central part of Bhutanese society and culture. The country's government is committed to preserving and promoting the Buddhist heritage of the country, and there are numerous festivals and religious celebrations throughout the year that highlight the importance of Buddhism in Bhutanese life.

Despite its central role in Bhutanese society, Buddhism in Bhutan faces a range of challenges, including declining monastic populations and a need to adapt to a rapidly changing world. However, the importance of Buddhism to the Bhutanese people and their way of life is likely to remain strong for many years to come.

The Traditional Arts and Crafts of Bhutan

The traditional arts and crafts of Bhutan are an important part of the country's cultural heritage. These crafts have been passed down through generations of Bhutanese artisans, and they play a significant role in the country's economy and identity.

Bhutanese traditional arts and crafts include a wide range of disciplines, including weaving, painting, carving, metalwork, and embroidery. These crafts are often closely linked to Bhutanese religious and cultural traditions, and they are characterized by their intricate designs and attention to detail.

One of the most famous Bhutanese crafts is weaving. Bhutanese weavers create a wide range of textiles, including the famous kira and gho garments worn by Bhutanese men and women. These textiles are made using a variety of techniques, including backstrap weaving, loom weaving, and supplementary weft weaving.

Another important Bhutanese craft is painting. Bhutanese painters create a wide range of religious and secular artworks, including thangkas (religious paintings on cloth), dzongs (fortresses), and chortens (stupas). These paintings are characterized by their vibrant colors and intricate details, and they often incorporate religious and mythological themes.

Carving is another important Bhutanese craft. Bhutanese carvers create a wide range of objects, including wooden bowls, masks, and religious sculptures. These carvings are often highly detailed and may incorporate religious or mythological themes.

Metalwork is another important Bhutanese craft. Bhutanese metalworkers create a wide range of objects, including traditional Bhutanese weapons, jewelry, and religious objects such as prayer wheels and bells. These objects are often highly ornate and may incorporate intricate designs and religious symbolism.

Embroidery is another important Bhutanese craft. Bhutanese embroiderers create a wide range of textiles, including clothing, tapestries, and religious banners. These textiles are often highly detailed and may incorporate a range of traditional Bhutanese designs and motifs.

Today, the traditional arts and crafts of Bhutan continue to play an important role in the country's economy and cultural identity. The Bhutanese government has implemented a range of policies aimed at preserving and promoting these crafts, including the establishment of training programs and the creation of markets and exhibitions for Bhutanese craftspeople.

Despite these efforts, the traditional arts and crafts of Bhutan face a range of challenges, including competition from mass-produced goods and a need to adapt to changing consumer tastes. However, the importance of these crafts to the Bhutanese people and their cultural heritage is likely to remain strong for many years to come.

The Festivals and Celebrations of Bhutan

Bhutan is known for its vibrant and colorful festivals and celebrations. These festivals are an important part of Bhutanese culture and traditions, and they play a significant role in the country's social and religious life.

Bhutanese festivals are often linked to Buddhist or animist traditions and are held throughout the year. These festivals are known as tshechus and are typically celebrated in honor of Guru Rinpoche, a Buddhist saint who brought Buddhism to Bhutan in the 8th century.

Tshechus are typically held in the courtyards of Bhutanese monasteries or dzongs and are characterized by their vibrant colors, traditional dances, and elaborate costumes. The dances performed during tshechus often tell religious or mythological stories and are performed by monks or laypeople.

One of the most famous tshechus in Bhutan is the Paro Tsechu, which is held annually in Paro in the spring. This festival attracts thousands of visitors from around the world and is known for its elaborate dances and colorful costumes.

Another important festival in Bhutan is the Punakha Drubchen, which is held in the Punakha Dzong in the winter. This festival is known for its reenactment of a famous battle that took place in the 17th century and is characterized by its masked dances and traditional music.

Other festivals in Bhutan include the Wangdue Phodrang Tshechu, the Thimphu Tsechu, and the Haa Summer Festival. These festivals are celebrated throughout the year and provide a unique opportunity to experience Bhutanese culture and traditions firsthand.

In addition to the tshechus, Bhutanese also celebrate a range of other cultural and religious festivals throughout the year. These festivals may be linked to animist or Hindu traditions and often involve traditional music, dance, and food.

One of the most important non-Buddhist festivals in Bhutan is the annual Black-Necked Crane Festival, which is held in the Phobjikha Valley in the fall. This festival celebrates the arrival of the endangered black-necked cranes and is characterized by its traditional songs, dances, and handicrafts.

Today, the festivals and celebrations of Bhutan continue to play an important role in the country's cultural identity and tourism industry. The Bhutanese government is committed to preserving and promoting these festivals and has implemented a range of policies aimed at ensuring their continued success and sustainability.

The Architecture of Bhutan

Bhutan is known for its unique and distinctive architecture, which reflects the country's rich cultural and religious heritage. The traditional architecture of Bhutan is characterized by its use of natural materials, intricate woodwork, and decorative painting.

The most iconic architectural structures in Bhutan are the dzongs, which are fortified monasteries that serve as administrative and religious centers. Dzongs are typically built on high ground and are surrounded by thick walls and watchtowers. These structures were traditionally used for defense against invading forces, but today they serve as important cultural and religious sites.

The architecture of Bhutan is heavily influenced by Buddhist beliefs and principles. Traditional Bhutanese architecture emphasizes harmony with the natural environment and the use of natural materials. This is reflected in the use of local stone, wood, and earth in construction, as well as in the incorporation of natural elements into the design of buildings.

Bhutanese architecture also incorporates intricate woodwork and decorative painting, which are used to adorn the exteriors and interiors of buildings. The use of vibrant colors and patterns in painting is particularly striking and is used to convey spiritual and religious themes.

The traditional architecture of Bhutan is also notable for its use of large, sloping roofs that provide shelter from the elements and help to regulate temperature. The roofs are typically supported by wooden beams and are covered in wooden shingles or slabs of slate.

In addition to dzongs, Bhutanese architecture also includes a variety of other traditional structures such as farmhouses, temples, and bridges. These structures also feature the same distinctive elements of natural materials, intricate woodwork, and decorative painting.

Today, Bhutanese architecture is undergoing a transformation as the country modernizes and urbanizes. While traditional elements are still incorporated into new buildings, modern materials such as concrete and steel are also being used. However, the government of Bhutan is committed to preserving traditional architecture and has implemented policies to ensure that new construction conforms to traditional design principles.

In conclusion, the architecture of Bhutan is a unique and important aspect of the country's cultural heritage. The use of natural materials, intricate woodwork, and decorative painting reflects Bhutanese values of harmony with the environment and spiritual significance. While traditional architecture is facing challenges in the modern era, the government and people of Bhutan remain committed to preserving and promoting this important cultural tradition.

The Impact of Tourism on Bhutan

Tourism has had a significant impact on the small Himalayan kingdom of Bhutan. Since opening its borders to foreign tourists in 1974, the country has seen a steady increase in the number of visitors, with tourism now a major source of revenue for the country. While the growth of the tourism industry has brought economic benefits to Bhutan, it has also had social, cultural, and environmental impacts that must be carefully managed.

Economic Impact: Tourism is a major contributor to Bhutan's economy, accounting for over 10% of the country's GDP. The industry has created jobs and stimulated economic growth, particularly in the service sector. The government has implemented policies to ensure that tourism revenue benefits the country as a whole, with a portion of the revenue going towards education, healthcare, and infrastructure development.

Social Impact: Tourism has had a significant impact on Bhutanese society, particularly in terms of the exposure to different cultures and lifestyles. Tourism has brought new ideas and perspectives to the country, and has helped to create a more cosmopolitan society. However, there have also been concerns about the impact of tourism on traditional Bhutanese culture, particularly the risk of cultural commodification and erosion.

Cultural Impact: The traditional culture of Bhutan is one of the country's biggest draws for tourists. However, the influx of tourists has raised concerns about the impact of tourism on cultural authenticity. There have been concerns that tourism has commodified Bhutanese culture and that the authenticity of Bhutanese traditions is being lost. To address these concerns, the government has implemented policies to ensure that tourism is sustainable and that cultural heritage is preserved.

Environmental Impact: Tourism has had a significant impact on the environment in Bhutan. The increase in the number of tourists has led to increased demand for resources, particularly energy, water, and waste management services. Additionally, the development of tourism infrastructure has led to habitat loss and degradation. To address these concerns, the government has implemented policies to ensure that tourism development is sustainable and that the environment is protected.

Tourism has had a significant impact on Bhutan, both positive and negative. While the industry has brought economic benefits, it has also raised concerns about social, cultural, and environmental impacts. The government of Bhutan has implemented policies to ensure that tourism is sustainable and that the benefits of tourism are distributed fairly across the country. The impact of tourism on Bhutan will continue to be a topic of discussion as the country navigates the challenges and opportunities presented by this growing industry.

Bhutan's Environmental Conservation Efforts

Bhutan is a small country with a unique focus on environmental conservation. The country has prioritized environmental conservation as a national policy, recognizing the importance of preserving its unique environment and biodiversity. Bhutan's efforts in environmental conservation are largely driven by its commitment to Gross National Happiness, which emphasizes the importance of sustainable development and environmental stewardship.

Bhutan's Constitution includes a requirement that the country maintain a minimum of 60% forest cover. Currently, Bhutan's forest cover is estimated at 71%, one of the highest in the world. The country has implemented various policies and programs to maintain its forest cover and preserve its biodiversity.

One of the main strategies for environmental conservation in Bhutan is the establishment of protected areas. The country has set aside a significant portion of its land as protected areas, including national parks, wildlife sanctuaries, and nature reserves. These protected areas are managed by the Department of Forests and Park Services and serve as important habitats for endangered species, such as the Bengal tiger and the snow leopard.

Another key aspect of Bhutan's environmental conservation efforts is sustainable land use practices. The country has implemented various programs to promote sustainable agriculture, including organic farming and agroforestry.

The government has also launched a program to promote the use of renewable energy sources, including solar, wind, and hydroelectric power, to reduce the country's dependence on fossil fuels.

Bhutan is also actively involved in global efforts to address climate change. The country has committed to remaining carbon neutral and has implemented various initiatives to reduce greenhouse gas emissions. The Bhutan for Life initiative, launched in 2017, aims to create a sustainable financing mechanism for the country's protected areas, helping to ensure their long-term conservation.

Bhutan's environmental conservation efforts have been recognized internationally, with the country receiving multiple awards for its commitment to sustainability. The country has been hailed as a model for environmental conservation and sustainable development, with many countries looking to Bhutan as an example to follow.

Bhutan's environmental conservation efforts are driven by the country's unique focus on Gross National Happiness, sustainable development, and environmental stewardship. The country's commitment to maintaining a minimum of 60% forest cover and its establishment of protected areas have helped to preserve its unique biodiversity. Bhutan's promotion of sustainable land use practices and renewable energy sources are also important components of its environmental conservation efforts. The country's dedication to environmental conservation has earned it international recognition and serves as an example for other countries seeking to balance economic development with environmental sustainability.

Bhutan's Future and its Role in the Global Community

Bhutan has come a long way since its inception as a modern nation-state in the early 20th century. Today, the country has made significant progress in areas such as environmental conservation, education, and economic development. As Bhutan looks to the future, it faces both challenges and opportunities, both domestically and globally.

One of the main challenges facing Bhutan is its need for economic development. Despite its progress in areas such as environmental conservation and education, the country remains one of the least developed in the world. While the government has launched various initiatives to promote economic growth, such as the Bhutan Economic Forum for Innovative Transformation, there is still much work to be done to address issues such as poverty and unemployment.

At the same time, Bhutan's unique focus on Gross National Happiness, which emphasizes the importance of environmental sustainability and social well-being, has gained international recognition. The country's commitment to environmental conservation and sustainable development has inspired other countries to adopt similar policies and practices.

Bhutan's role in the global community is also growing, with the country becoming increasingly engaged in regional and international affairs. Bhutan is a member of various international organizations, such as the United Nations and the South Asian Association for Regional Cooperation, and has played an active role in promoting peace and cooperation in the region. In addition, Bhutan has developed strong diplomatic relations with countries such as India, China, and Japan.

Looking to the future, Bhutan faces both opportunities and challenges. The country's unique approach to development, which emphasizes environmental sustainability and social well-being, offers valuable lessons for the rest of the world. However, Bhutan will need to continue to address issues such as economic development and poverty reduction if it is to fully realize its potential.

Bhutan's future is shaped by both domestic and global factors. The country's unique focus on Gross National Happiness, environmental sustainability, and social well-being has gained international recognition and has inspired other countries to adopt similar policies and practices. Bhutan's role in the global community is also growing, with the country becoming increasingly engaged in regional and international affairs. However, Bhutan still faces challenges such as economic development and poverty reduction, which will need to be addressed in order for the country to fully realize its potential.

Conclusion

Bhutan is a small, landlocked country located in the eastern Himalayas. Despite its size and relative isolation, Bhutan has a rich and fascinating history, with a unique culture and society that has evolved over centuries. In recent decades, Bhutan has also emerged as a leader in environmental conservation and sustainable development, with its emphasis on Gross National Happiness gaining international recognition.

Throughout this book, we have explored the different aspects of Bhutan's history, culture, society, and environment. We have traced the country's early settlements and the arrival of Buddhism, explored the formation of early kingdoms and the emergence of the monarchy, and examined the impact of colonialism and modernization on Bhutanese society. We have also explored the role of religion, arts, and festivals in Bhutanese culture, as well as the country's unique approach to governance and development.

One of the key themes that emerges from our exploration of Bhutan's history and society is the country's emphasis on the principles of Gross National Happiness. This approach, which emphasizes the importance of environmental sustainability, social well-being, and cultural preservation, has become a defining feature of Bhutan's identity and has gained international recognition. By focusing on the well-being of its citizens and the preservation of its natural and cultural heritage, Bhutan has demonstrated that there are alternative paths to development that prioritize human welfare and environmental sustainability.

However, Bhutan also faces a number of challenges as it looks to the future. The country is still one of the least developed in the world, with high levels of poverty and unemployment. At the same time, Bhutan's rapid economic growth and increasing engagement with the global community bring with them new challenges, such as environmental degradation and cultural change.

Despite these challenges, Bhutan's future looks promising. The country's commitment to Gross National Happiness and environmental conservation offers a unique perspective on development that can inspire other countries to pursue more sustainable and equitable paths. Bhutan's growing engagement with the global community also offers new opportunities for the country to share its experiences and learn from others.

In conclusion, Bhutan is a remarkable country with a rich and unique history, culture, and environment. By embracing the principles of Gross National Happiness and prioritizing environmental sustainability, social well-being, and cultural preservation, Bhutan has become a global leader in sustainable development. As the country looks to the future, it will need to continue to address the challenges it faces, but its commitment to these principles offers hope and inspiration to people around the world.

Thank you for taking the time to read this book on the history of Bhutan. We hope that it has provided you with an informative and engaging journey through the country's fascinating past and present.

We would greatly appreciate it if you could leave a positive review of the book on the platform where you purchased it. Your feedback and support will help other readers discover the book and also encourage us to continue creating high-quality content in the future.

Thank you once again for your interest in Bhutan and its history. We hope that this book has inspired you to learn more about this unique and remarkable country.

Printed in Great Britain
by Amazon

46085905R00036